MY PARENTS ARE DIVORCING.
NOW WHAT?

PAULA MORROW

ROSEN
PUBLISHING®

New York

Published in 2015 by The Rosen Publishing Group, Inc.
29 East 21st Street, New York, NY 10010

Library of Congress Cataloging-in-Publication Data

Morrow, Paula.
My parents are divorcing. Now what?/Paula Morrow.—
First edition.
        pages cm.—(Teen life 411)
Includes bibliographical references and index.
ISBN 978-1-4777-7986-6 (library bound)
1. Divorce—Juvenile literature. 2. Children of divorced
parents—Juvenile literature. 3. Divorced parents—Juvenile
literature. 4. Teenagers—Family relationships—Juvenile
literature. I. Title.
HQ814.M67 2014
306.89—dc23
                                                    2014014182

Manufactured in China

CONTENTS

Your life is about to change permanently. Your parents have told you they are going to get a divorce.

Maybe you've seen the signs and hoped you were wrong. Or maybe the announcement came as a total surprise to you. But now it's real. You feel like the ground just collapsed under your feet.

You're filled with questions: What's going to happen to me? Where will I live? Will I have to change schools? How do I tell my friends? Am I a failure?

"Is it my fault?"

The first thing to do is settle that last question. No, it's not your fault. The reasons for your parents' divorce—whatever those reasons may be—are between the two of them. You are never responsible for your parents' actions.

After your heart stops pounding and you can take a deep breath, the second thing to know is that you can cope. No matter how dire life may seem right now, the earth is still turning, and the sun will come up tomorrow morning. The majority of parents

Your parents are always angry. You hate hearing them yell at each other. But no matter how bad it gets, you don't really want them to divorce.

are able to have an ongoing, loving relationship with their children after a divorce. And the majority of children with divorced parents can go on to have happy and successful lives.

A lot depends on your personality and support network. Your personality was formed a long time ago, in your preschool years. You already have a good idea whether you're shy or outgoing, cautious or impulsive, logical or emotional, and many other features of your personality. These traits will affect how you respond to the divorce. There's no "right" or "wrong" here; you are who you are. Focus on your personal strengths, and when you're feeling down, remind yourself what's good about you.

Your support network is made up of people you trust who care about you. You're going through a rough patch, and you will need emotional and practical support though the coming weeks and months. Don't try to go it alone; allow yourself to accept support when it is offered and ask for it when it is not.

You are not alone. According to the National Center for Health Statistics, there are more than one million divorces in the United States every year. The majority of divorces occur in families with children under the age of eighteen. The 2010 Census reported over twenty-four million minor teens (ages twelve to seventeen) in the United States Of those, more than six million lived with their mother only; more than one million lived with their father only. Another one and a half million weren't with either parent; they lived with grandparents, other relatives, friends, or foster families.

That means a lot of other kids and teens have faced what you're facing. You probably have friends with divorced parents, friends who can help you get through this.

There are also other adults in your community besides your parents you can turn to, adults who can be part of your support network. They might be neighbors, teachers, coaches, counselors, people at your place of worship, or parents of your friends.

Many organizations provide information and support. Interactive websites let you ask questions, join chat rooms, read what other people your age are saying, offer your own comments, find tips on ways to cope, and get advice from professionals. Some toll-free telephone hotlines have counselors available 24/7 to respond if you need to talk with someone immediately.

Your parents are divorcing each other, but you still have a family. After all, families aren't defined by who lives where. Families are people who love and care for each other.

CHAPTER 1

THE "D" WORD

Your parents have said it: the "D" word. It's hanging in the air, naked and ugly, and there is no way to un-say it. Your parents have announced that they are going to get a divorce.

Some parents have been fighting for years, so you're used to hearing them yelling at each other. You don't like it, but it seems normal. On the other hand, some parents never fight in front of you and have been hiding their problems, so you had no clue anything was wrong. Either way, you don't want to hear your own parents use the "D" word.

All parents disagree from time to time. Maybe you wish yours wouldn't fight so much, but they're still your parents, and this is your home.

COMMON REACTIONS

Everyone is different, and no one else will have exactly the same combination of thoughts and feelings that you have right now. But everyone who has ever gone through this news has shared some similar reactions. It can be helpful to have an idea what to expect. You may feel some or all of these. Remember that there are no "right" or "wrong" feelings. Your feelings are normal for you. What's important is how you deal with those feelings.

"How Could They Do This to Me?"

Parents have a special responsibility in this world: It's their job to take care of their children. From the tiny honeybees carefully tending baby bees in their hives to the huge elephant herds forming a circle around their calves when a predator approaches, parents instinctively put the safety, security, and welfare of their young above their own lives. Now, suddenly, your parents seem to be throwing your security out the window.

It's natural to feel a sense of betrayal. One little girl, after her father moved out, wrote him a letter asking who would fix her bike if it broke. What she was really asking was, "Don't you care what happens to me?" Even when you get older and know where to get your bike fixed (or your car or whatever else might break), there's still that awful sense that the absent parent has abandoned you.

In a way, the parent who did not leave may also seem to be abandoning you emotionally. He or she may be distant or preoccupied—indifferent to your pain and unresponsive to your needs. Sometimes it's hard to know what hurts more, the physical absence or the emotional absence.

Believe it or not, neither parent has really abandoned you. Their differences are with each other, not with you. They're splitting up from each other, not from you. When a marriage fails, the spouses often feel like failures, too. They may be embarrassed or ashamed to talk with you. They may feel helpless to "fix it," so they don't say or do anything.

You might stop reading here and try to think of a reason one or both of your parents could have for acting distant—a reason that doesn't have anything to do with you.

"Whose Fault Was It?"

When things go wrong, it's human instinct to wonder why. We're hard-wired that way; it's how we learn. Many questions, however, don't have easy answers, and some have no answers at all. Trying to blame the divorce on one parent or the other—or both of them—is a dead-end street. It will get you nowhere.

The urge to place blame can be even stronger if it appears that one or the other parent has done something bad that triggered the divorce. Resist that urge. Despite everything you may see or hear, it's a safe bet that you don't know the whole story. Parents have a history that goes back before you were born, and they have lives of their own beyond their relationship with you.

Parents and their children don't always agree on everything. You may have argued with a parent, but that would never cause the parent to leave home.

In the book *How I Became a Ghost* by Tim Tingle, a young Choctaw boy tells of being forced from his home on the Trail of Tears. Looking back, he sees bloody footprints left by his bare feet on the snow. His father tells him to look just once at the trail behind him, acknowledging the struggle, and then to face forward and keep walking. It's a great analogy. In the days and weeks ahead, you may at times feel as if you're leaving bloody footprints in the snow. Acknowledge that feeling; admit that you're hurting. Then turn and look forward. Ahead of you, the snow will be clean.

When things get bad, it's tempting to give up. Your inner voices may tell you you're worthless. That's not true. The divorce is not your fault.

"What Did I Do Wrong?"

Have you ever argued with your parents? Have you ever broken a rule or come home late or failed to do a chore or disappointed your parents in any way? Of course you have—it's called being human. That is not the reason your parents are getting a divorce.

Part of growing from a child to a young adult is learning to think for yourself and to form your own opinions. It's natural that some of those thoughts and opinions will be different from those of your parents. This can lead to disagreements, maybe even fights, but it does not cause a parent to move out.

HOW TO MAKE DECISIONS WHEN YOU DON'T FEEL LIKE DECIDING

- Try to buy yourself some time. Unless it's an urgent decision that must be made immediately, it's fine to say, "I'm not ready to answer that yet. Let me get back to you."
- Ask questions to be sure you understand your choices. Don't be pressured into agreeing to (or rejecting) something you don't understand.
- Mentally (or on paper if you prefer) list all your options; consider the advantages and drawbacks of each one.
- Cross off the options that you like least. It helps to see the list get shorter.
- The old "scale of 1 to 10" trick still works. Ask yourself, "On a scale of 1 to 10, how strongly do I feel about this option?" Focus on the options with the highest numbers.
- Do two options seem equal? Sometimes it helps to turn the question around to see which one you want less. Pretend someone else decided for you and chose option B instead of option A. How disappointed are you?

You may have heard your parents arguing about you when they thought you couldn't hear them. They might not agree about your curfew or your allowance or a dozen other things. Maybe you've even taken advantage of their differences, asking one parent for something you want when you know the other would say no. Don't worry; the divorce is still not your fault. In a strong marriage, spouses stay together and work through such disagreements. In a weak marriage, even if there are no obvious disagreements over parenting, other issues between the spouses arise and lead to divorce.

If you think the divorce is partly or entirely your fault, that idea will eat away at your self-esteem. You may hear your inner voice saying: "Your own parents don't even love you. You're completely worthless."

Don't listen to it.

Your parents are not divorcing because of you. No matter how unhappy with you a parent may have been, you are not the reason he or she moved out of the house.

"Why Do I Even Try?"

When life is spinning out of control, it's tempting to give up. Sometimes people who are in a bad place emotionally may sabotage themselves. They don't do it on purpose, but unconsciously they feel things are going to go bad anyway. When they make poor decisions that cause further problems, they can say, "See, I knew it would go wrong."

Something as major as a divorce can ruin your judgment. You may find yourself making bad or harmful choices. They could be about anything, not just things that are related to the divorce: "I can wear this shirt to school one more day. It doesn't smell *that* bad, and nobody cares what I look like." "I don't feel like studying for the test. I'm going to flunk anyway."

It may feel like you have no control in life, but in reality, you still have a lot of control. It's all about choices and consequences. There's nothing you can do about the past; what's done is done. But you have a future, and that future depends in part on the decisions you're making today. Even though you're not happy now, you can make choices that will help you be happier in the future.

It can help to bounce ideas off of a friend, a counselor, or someone else you know and trust. If you do ask someone else's opinion, you don't have to follow his or her advice. Consider what he or she says, but know that you can ignore it if it feels wrong to you. Remember, the decision you make today will still be important tomorrow.

Insensitive Things People Say

When you tell people your parents are getting a divorce, they don't always know what to say. Sometimes they want to be sympathetic, but the words come out wrong and sound hurtful instead. Don't be offended by these well-meaning but tone-deaf remarks. Try to look beyond what they said and turn it into an idea that's healthy and helpful.

"You're Better Off Without Him/Her."

This is an insensitive remark that not only insults your absent parent, but also attacks whatever happy memories you have of the time when your parents were together.

You may be angry with your parent, but that doesn't mean you want or need to hear an outsider speak badly of him or her. Ignore the criticism implied in this remark. Instead, you can look for the positives. You may not be better off without one of your parents in the household, but now you no longer live in an atmosphere of anger and hostility. Without the daily conflict, you can forge a positive one-on-one relationship with each of your parents. You no longer have to deal with so much of the burden of your parents' failing relationship.

"You're Learning from This Experience."

This cynical comment seems to imply that you're so dumb that bad things have to happen to wake you up. It also seems to imply that you're somehow to blame for the divorce: It happened to teach you a lesson. No, neither statement is true. Life is not like Aesop's fables, where every story has a moral lesson. Life happens. You can choose to learn from this experience or not, just as you choose whether to learn from every other experience you have.

"Wow, What Happened? Was Your Dad/Mom Having an Affair?"

The reasons for the divorce are nobody else's business, and you can totally ignore this question and any others

Friends and others who hear your parents are divorcing may not know what to say. Their comments may sound rude or hurtful or just plain dumb. You don't owe them any explanation.

that invite gossip. Your life is not a soap opera for someone else's entertainment.

You don't have to be rude in return; you can rise above that. If you feel a need to answer out loud, the best choice is a non-answer such as, "I don't think that should concern you," said in a firm but not unfriendly voice. It may be tempting to be sarcastic, but resist the temptation. A mud fight just gets everyone dirty, and it's the last thing you need to complicate your life.

"You'll Get Over It."

This assurance is incredibly naive. Divorce is never "over." Your parents will be divorced from each other for the rest of your life. They may move or get married to someone else or introduce new people into your extended family. These changes are not going to go away. What will go away, fortunately, is the sharp emotional pain that distracts you all day and keeps you awake at night. In time, the divorce will become background to your life, rather than the central focus. A wise young woman once walked into a support group meeting and introduced herself by saying, "I'm Mary, and I expect to reach the point where this is not the only thing I can talk about." You will reach that point, too.

MYTHS AND FACTS

MYTH

Half of all marriages end in divorce.

FACT

Census data does show that the number of people who get divorced in a year is about half the number of people who get married in a year. However, this statistic is misleading. The marriage figures show only the number of people in the country who got married in a single year. The divorce figures include all people who divorced in that year, regardless of whether they had been married for one year or much longer.

MYTH

You'll have to choose between your mom and your dad.

FACT

You have the right to love and have a relationship with both parents. Regardless of who has custody, you have the right to see the noncustodial parent regularly. But you do not choose who will have custody or where you will live; the judge who grants the divorce will make those decisions. If you have a strong opinion, you'll be allowed to say so, either to the judge directly or to a court-appointed advocate. Still, the final decision rests with the judge.

MYTH

There's nothing you can do about it.

FACT

You can choose how you will react. The divorce is between your parents, and you can't prevent it, but you don't have to let it ruin your life. You can tell each parent what you need from him or her. You can maintain a healthy relationship with each parent separately. You can protect your own well-being and happiness.

MYTHS AND FACTS

CHAPTER 2

THE GRIEVING PROCESS

There's another word that people don't like to talk about: death. In many ways, divorce taps into similar emotions. It's the end of your life as you've known it so far. The good news is that divorce is not fatal—but knowing it won't kill you doesn't necessarily comfort you while it's happening. Allow yourself to mourn what you are losing.

THE STAGES OF GRIEF

In the 1960s, a doctor named Elisabeth Kübler-Ross began talking with hospital patients who were dying. She identified five stages of grief, which can also be applied to other forms of loss besides death. You will probably feel some or all of these emotions as you grieve the loss of the family you have always known. In fact, you may continue to feel some of them for months or even years after your parents' divorce. Recognizing that these feelings are normal and that you are still a good person can help you heal.

Denial

Even if you suspected things weren't right, it's still a shock when your parents announce that they are getting divorced. Your first thought may be, "They don't mean it. They're just mad." Or you may think, "They mean it right now, but they'll get over it. They won't really do it."

By the time your parents announce their plan to divorce, they have had a lot of time to think and talk about it. Chances are that you didn't know about these private conversations. When you hear about the divorce, things are already in motion. Your parents still might change their minds and stay together, but you shouldn't pin your hopes on that happening.

Denial is your mind's way of adjusting to terrible news. When something is too much to handle all at once, you need time to absorb the information little by little. You don't have to say or do anything right away. If someone asks what you think, it's OK to say, "I don't know yet," or "Give me time to adjust to the idea."

As the fact of the divorce slowly sinks in, try to think beyond how unacceptable it is. It might help to focus on small details, rather than the whole overwhelming picture. Not "My parents are splitting up forever," but "I'll have two homes now. I'm going to need two tooth-brushes." The small details can make the experience more manageable.

This trick of dealing with small, manageable details can be a useful coping mechanism as time goes on, too. Some people slip back into denial long after they think they've adjusted to a disaster. Any time you start to feel like you can't cope, step back from the big situation and look for some small area in which you do have con-trol—even if it's only a toothbrush.

When a disaster is too much to handle all at once, your mind may simply shut out the news. Temporary denial is a way of coping that lets you adjust gradually.

Anger

Go ahead and get mad. After all, until now, your parents were committed to raising you and your siblings together, to providing a home and taking care of you until you grow up and are ready to have a home of your own. Suddenly one or both of your parents reneged on the deal. Is that fair? No. Of course you're mad.

(And if you're not mad, that can be a form of denial.)

Just remember, it's OK to get mad—but it's not OK to stay mad forever. That will eat you up inside. At first your anger may hurt the person you're mad at, but in time it will hurt you even more.

Anger can show up in many different ways. You might not feel anger directly toward your parents. Perhaps there's someone else you blame: Dad's boss who fired him; Mom's sick sister who demanded so much attention; your bratty little brother. Or perhaps a third person got in the middle of your parents' marriage and messed things up. If you want someone to be mad at, that's a great candidate.

Anger can spill over onto people and things that have nothing at all to do with the divorce. You may feel angry with teachers who give too much homework, with slow store clerks, with strangers who get in your way. You may be mad at your friends for not taking your parents' divorce seriously enough and wanting to go on as usual—or for taking it too seriously and treating you as if you have a fatal disease.

Anger can cause you to resent kids your age whose parents are still together. Why should they still have a life when yours is falling to pieces?

Don't let anyone tell you not to be mad. Just like denial, anger is a perfectly normal response. It's OK to have angry feelings. The important thing is to deal with them in a way that's healthy for you. Otherwise all that adrenaline will just churn around in your body and cause you even more problems. You need to deal with your anger in a way that won't hurt you or anyone else.

Anger and resentment can build up inside until you feel like a witch's cauldron of seething emotions. Anger is normal. There are ways to let it out so that it won't eat you up inside.

First, recognize your anger; don't try to ignore it. Second, when you feel that rush of anger, try to understand exactly what made you mad. Identifying the reason is a way to move toward coping with it.

There's something called the "broken cookie syndrome." Imagine a five-year-old having a bad day. He spills his breakfast all over his favorite shirt and has to change clothes before going to kindergarten. He falls down on the playground and skins his knees. Other kids laugh at him. Through it all, he's silent and brave. After school, his mom gives him a big chocolate chip cookie, but he drops it on the floor and it breaks into crumbs. Suddenly he starts screaming and crying. Is he crying about the cookie? Of course not. He's crying about everything that happened all day, the hurts he's been holding inside. The broken cookie is simply the trigger.

You may suddenly find yourself furious over something that seems minor, and people will tell you that you're overreacting. If you can identify what's really wrong, you can keep your anger from damaging relationships and driving away your friends.

While it's OK to get mad, it only hurts you to stay mad for very long. If you feel angry for more than a week or two, you may need outside help to deal with it. A trained counselor or other trustworthy adult can help you get through it.

Anger is an emotion, but it's definitely physical as well. It makes your heart pound, your temperature rise, your face get red, your breathing race, and your muscles tighten. Some of your best responses are physical, too.

You can channel all that angry energy—perhaps through sports or another extracurricular activity you enjoy—to help instead of hurt yourself.

Bargaining

We live in a capitalistic society. Everything has a price, whether it's cash, credit, trade, or something else. You can't exactly buy good health, but you can buy medicines and pay a doctor to make you better when you're sick. Even friendships involve trade-offs: I let you pick the movies we see, and you help me with my math homework.

Vigorous physical activity is a great way to get rid of all the adrenaline building up in your body and to work out those churning, angry feelings.

It's natural, then, to turn to bargaining as a way to control problems. It works with small things: "If I can use your car tonight, I promise to be home before midnight." Why not big things? "If I do all my chores without complaining, Mom and Dad won't split up."

Or if you know that the divorce is inevitable, you may find yourself bargaining about the terms: "If I bring my grades up, Mom and Dad will stay together until I graduate and come to the ceremony together."

Do you see a pattern here? Bargaining becomes a way of trying to take responsibility for keeping your parents together. But it won't work.

The trouble with bargaining in this way is that it's like trying to spend euros in an ice cream shop in Kansas. The currency doesn't match. Doing your chores has nothing to do with your parents' divorce, and neither does anything else you might offer. The decision to divorce is between your parents, and they're the only ones with "capital" to change that decision.

Depression

Everyone feels depressed from time to time. The word can mean "disappointed," as in "I'm depressed that you can't come to my party." It can mean "sorry," as in "I'm depressed that I spilled soda on your keyboard." It can simply mean "sad."

There's a depression, though, that's deeper and much more serious than simply feeling sad. It's a form of giving up. Often this happens when it hits you that the situation is real, that the divorce is going to happen, and that there's nothing you can do about it. A person who feels powerless may feel that the only response is "I don't care," as if shutting down your feelings will stop the hurt.

It's true that if you're numb, you can't feel pain. But if you're numb, you can't feel pleasure, either. No matter how bad things get, you can look for good in your life.

- Feeling extremely powerless or hopeless about the future
- Feeling worthless as a person
- Loss of interest in activities and things you used to enjoy
- Apathy toward friends, family, and others you used to care about
- Major change in appetite: eating much more or much less than usual
- Difficulty concentrating
- Major change in sleep habits: insomnia or excessive sleeping
- Major increase in use of medications, alcohol, or drugs
- Urges to hurt yourself
- Thoughts of death and suicide

If you experience four or more of these signs, you may be depressed. Don't try to tough it out on your own. This is a good time to talk with a trained counselor or other adult you trust.

WARNING SIGNS OF DEPRESSION

By all means, allow yourself to mourn for your very real losses. It's natural to grieve over the loss of the home and family you've known. If the divorce means you have to move, you'll mourn the loss of friends or activities. You might also mourn the loss of the future

A trained counselor or therapist will listen to your concerns and help you work through your feelings in healthy ways. What you tell a professional counselor is confidential.

you were expecting, with both parents and a stable home. If your sadness is overwhelming, though, and you never have a break from it, you may be slipping into serious depression. Fortunately, help is available. Clinical depression is a disease, and it can be treated. Don't be hesitant about asking for help if you feel you need it.

Acceptance

Accepting something doesn't necessarily mean you'll be happy about it. Nobody expects you to be happy that your parents are divorcing. Acceptance simply means recognizing that something is a fact and moving forward from there with your life.

Acceptance can't be forced on you from outside. The old "like it or lump it" attitude doesn't work. Instead, acceptance will grow from the inside out. It can start out as an empty feeling: letting go of the denial and anger, admitting that bargaining doesn't work, and coming through the depression. When you can admit to yourself that your parents' divorce is inevitable, yet still look forward to your own future, you have reached acceptance.

Hope is an important aspect of all stages, but especially of this one. Acceptance doesn't deny that you are living through a difficult time. It doesn't deny your pain or ask you to "get over it." Acceptance acknowledges that the present is what it is yet still allows you to hope that the future will be better. By accepting instead of fighting against the situation, you can move forward toward healing and happiness.

Even after a divorce, you can have a good relationship with each of your parents. They aren't perfect, but they still love you, and you can love them, too.

CHAPTER 3

A divorce in the family means a lot of changes for everyone in the household. Some of the changes will be immediate and dramatic. Others may not be obvious at first but will become evident as time goes on and you adjust to a new reality.

IMMEDIATE CHANGES

While your parents may have been thinking about divorce for some time, it's possible they have not talked about it with you. You may not have much time to prepare for the ways your life will change right away.

Someone Moves

One of the first things to happen when a couple decides to divorce is that someone moves. In a few cases, both members of the couple stay in the home, but one moves to a spare bedroom. This is a temporary measure, often because there isn't money to pay for a second apartment or house. But sooner or later, one parent is going to move out.

Usually the children and teens in the family stay in their own home, and only the parent moves. However, the parent who leaves may insist on taking the children, especially if the home has become dangerous due to violence or substance abuse.

If you stay in your home, you'll see changes around the household. Suddenly there's only one adult to do all the things that used to be done by two, from planning and preparing meals to putting gas in the car. You may be asked to take on extra chores and spend more time helping to keep things going at home.

If you have to move to a different home, it may or may not be in your same school district. Changing schools is a major disruption, especially if it happens in the middle of the school year. It means leaving your friends, being the "new kid," and having to adjust to new classes and teachers and make new friends. Moving can affect your extracurricular activities, too, both at school and in your community. It may become difficult to get together with friends for activities or just to hang out.

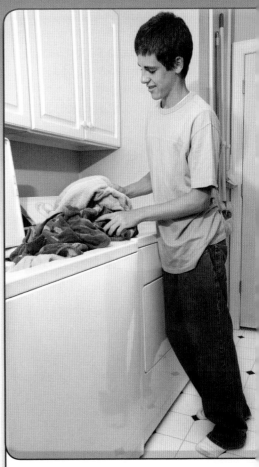

After a divorce, your single parent may have less time to do household chores while earning a living. You may find yourself taking up the slack around the house.

Money may be tight after a divorce. Finding a part-time job can give you your own spending money or even let you help with family expenses.

There's Less Money

A side effect of having someone move out is that the income that used to support your household suddenly is supporting two households. This is especially awkward because financial stress is one of the major contributors to divorce in the first place. A couple may have been fighting about money for a long time, and just when they need more to pay for a divorce, they actually have less.

The family budget is likely to get tighter. If you get an allowance, it may be reduced. If you're used to getting paid to do chores, you may suddenly be asked to do them as a contribution to the family, and perhaps even get a job yourself.

Not all legal aspects of a divorce will affect you. The most relevant ones for you are custody and visitation. But it's a good idea to understand the basics of other areas, too.

Your parents may start working longer hours to increase their income. If only one of your parents worked outside the home, chances are the stay-at-home parent will have to get a job to make ends meet. That puts more of a burden on you, too. Not only is there less cash for fun things, but also the parent with a new job won't be around as much and you'll have to take up the slack. For example, you may find yourself babysitting for younger siblings.

LEGAL ASPECTS

Divorce is a legal action, and many of the changes in your life will be outlined in legal

documents. That means you'll need to understand a lot of things you never wanted to hear, much less think about.

Separation

When one parent moves out of the home, that's clearly a physical separation, but it may or may not be a legal separation. There are two kinds of separation: trial separation and judicial separation.

A trial separation is when married spouses live separately for a specified period of time. This is an informal agreement and doesn't require the couple to go to court. In fact, it's sort of like a "time-out" for a couple that's having problems. The trial separation agreement states things like who will pay the bills and who will live with the children during the separation. The spouses haven't decided to get a divorce; they're just trying to see whether being apart from each other is better than being married. A period apart can help them clear their thinking. After this trial period, they may discover that they want to get back together, or they may decide that they no longer want to be married to each other.

A judicial separation is a legal decree that the couple will stop living together while their attorneys work out the details of a divorce. The judicial separation doesn't end the marriage, but it's a step in that direction.

Some couples separate without going on to get a divorce, but they have no intention of getting back together. They may have practical reasons to stay legally married, such as tax benefits or sharing health insurance, but still know that they never want to live together again. This can make their kids feel like they're in limbo. The best way to protect yourself emotionally is to think of them as being "practically divorced."

Custody

Probably the most important issue for you personally is custody because it will determine so many aspects of your life as long as you are a minor. While the laws are not exactly the same from state to state, they generally cover two things: where you will live and how decisions concerning you will be made.

Physical custody determines where you will live. If one parent has sole custody (or primary custody), you'll spend most of your time with that parent, who is called the "custodial" parent. You'll visit the other parent, the "noncustodial" parent.

If your parents have joint custody (also called "shared custody"), you will probably spend about the same amount of time with each parent. This works best if your parents live close to each other so that you can stay in one school with the same friends and activities and keep a fairly normal routine. It's possible for parents to have joint custody even if they live far apart, although this takes more effort to work well.

Joint custody can have a variety of forms. You may split weeks between your parents' homes or alternate longer periods between your two homes. You might spend weekdays with one parent, weekends and holidays with the other. There's even "bird's nest custody," in which you would stay in your home full-time and your parents alternate living there with you.

Legal custody determines who makes decisions about your life, regardless of where you live. These decisions could be about your education, religious upbringing, health care, discipline, schedule, and other things related to your needs. In most states, legal custody is usually shared by both parents, even if one parent has sole physical custody.

Visitation

Visitation is the time you spend with the noncustodial parent. You may stay at that parent's residence, go to visit other relatives, take a vacation together, or do whatever you and your parent would like to do during your visitation time.

Supervised visitation may be ordered by the judge if there is a risk of danger to you. Most often this happens because the noncustodial parent has a history of abuse, alcoholism, drug use, or violence. In this case, you would not be alone with the parent but would have another adult present for your protection. The visitation is likely to take place in a neutral location, rather than the noncustodial parent's residence.

Your Rights

In most cases, the judge will consider your preference for custody, along with all the other factors involved, but he or she will not necessarily agree with what you want.

Custody arrangements are primarily focused on clarifying the rights of each parent. The custody order

While no single, legally binding "Bill of Rights for Children of Divorce or Separation" exists, certain rights are important for your welfare and the health of your whole family. You and each of your parents should have such a list and be able to speak openly if you feel any of your rights are not being respected.

1. The right to be accepted and loved as a person, not a possession.
2. The right to love both parents and to express that love openly.
3. The right to have current contact information (address, phone, e-mail) for both parents.
4. The right to be welcome in both homes and to have your own private space in each home.
5. The right not to be forced to choose between your parents.
6. The right to have your questions answered honestly and respectfully.
7. The right to say "Stop!" if your parents fight in front of you.
8. The right not to hear one parent (or anyone else) bad-mouth the other.
9. The right not to be used as a go-between by your parents.
10. The right not to be used as a weapon in the divorce.
11. The right to know the custody arrangements.
12. The right to a copy of the visitation schedule.
13. The right to be told immediately of any changes that will affect you.
14. The right to see a counselor, therapist, or other professional if you want to.
15. The right to be loved unconditionally.

BILL OF RIGHTS FOR CHILDREN OF DIVORCE OR SEPARATION

includes the phrase "best interests of the child," but it does not spell out your rights in nearly as much detail as your parents' rights. A number of organizations have created lists of the rights of children caught in a divorce. While the lists differ, they all agree in certain areas. These lists are not legal documents in the same sense that a custody order is, but they clarify basic rights that every child of divorced or separated parents should have.

STEPFAMILIES

After your parents divorce, chances are good that one or both of them will start seeing other people. It will probably feel weird to have your parents dating when you might be dating, too. You may resent the fact that they seem to be moving on from each other so easily. This makes the divorce more real and takes away any hope you may have that they'll get back together.

It's even harder if you know or suspect that your parent's "someone special" was already on the scene before the divorce. In that case, you'll need to step back from the urge to judge or blame. Despite appearances, you can't know the whole story. Anger will only hurt you and prevent you from moving forward with your own life.

The National Stepfamily Resource Center estimates that about 75 percent of divorced people remarry, and about 65 percent of these marriages involve children from previous marriages. You are likely to find yourself part of a blended family, or stepfamily.

Stepmothers and Stepfathers

A stepparent is just a person like any other person. In other words, they're all different, so keep an open mind, no matter what stereotypes would have you believe.

Your parent may be eager for you to bond with your stepparent quickly, but that's not realistic. Don't expect to love your stepparent right away. Start by being civil. Friendship may grow slowly. Don't feel disloyal if you like your stepparent; he or she will never replace your own parent. Adding a new person to your life does not diminish your love for the people who are already there.

It might help to remember that your stepparent probably feels awkward and insecure, too. Your attitude can make that person's transition into your family smoother. Look for something to like or at least respect. If you can't, you can be neutral. Don't change yourself, and don't expect the other person to change, but be willing to meet halfway.

Getting to know each other can be especially difficult if you only see the stepparent during visitation with your noncustodial parent. You don't have as much time to adjust to each other. You may feel that the stepparent is intruding on your limited time with your parent. Try to spend a little of each visit talking with your stepparent. Be willing to be friendly. Then you can take some one-on-one time with your parent as well.

Your mother may be jealous of your stepmother, or your father may be jealous of your stepfather. By being open about your feelings, you can let them

Having a new stepfamily may mean you have to share your bedroom. Chances are your new stepsibling feels just as awkward and reluctant about that as you do.

know they have nothing to worry about. Resist the temptation to extravagantly praise or criticize the stepparent when you're at your other home.

Stepbrothers and Stepsisters

A new stepparent may come with strings attached in the form of stepbrothers and stepsisters. Here, again, it will take time to adjust to your new stepfamily. As you do, remember that your stepsiblings are hurting, too.

If you have to share a room, talk over how you can arrange it so that you each have some private space as well as the shared space. Respect the other person's needs as a way of showing how you'd like to be treated.

Finding common ground with stepsiblings can help you feel better about each other and yourself. For example, if stepsiblings are older than you are, pick a convenient time to ask for help or advice with something they're good at, or if they are anywhere close to your own age, get together for a fun activity. Keep an open mind—you might have more fun than you expect.

Don't let your stepsiblings boss you around. You can be gentle and firm at the same time. Don't yell or pout. Just treat them the way you wish they would treat you.

Strange as it seems, your parents may be part of the problem. You might hear them arguing about "your kids" and "my kids." Try to remember that this is a new situation for them, too, and they're going to make some mistakes. Wait for a time when you can talk to your parent quietly and explain how the arguments make you feel.

You may feel jealous of your stepsiblings. Would it surprise you to learn that they feel jealous of you, too? You've all had a major change in your life, and it's natural to feel unsettled. You may each have advantages that the others don't. Try to channel your jealousy into opportunities to share, support, and learn from each other.

Stepfamily Dynamics

Be prepared for personality conflicts. That's a normal part of being human. Don't let them seem magnified just because you're a stepfamily now. It's not worth fighting over small stuff. Look for something that you can admire about your stepparents or stepsiblings. Give a sincere compliment once in a while, even if it's simple.

When you're angry, it might be tempting to say something like, "You're not my real family." Not a good idea. Everyone in the family is aware of the relationships. Instead of "fightin' words," focus your argument on the specific issue at hand. State your case as calmly as you can, being firm but respectful.

While your new stepfamily may not be the family you would have chosen, it's the family you have. With a positive attitude, willingness to compromise, and the courage to stick up for yourself when necessary, you can make it work.

Ongoing Challenges

After the initial trauma of changes and adjustments, just when you start to think maybe life can go on, additional hassles can sneak up and hit you unexpectedly.

Two Homes

Keeping up with two homes can be a drag. You're late for school, and you realize you forgot your math book at your other house. A friend calls and asks you to come to a party, and the outfit you want to wear is in your other closet. If your parents can afford to buy you two of everything, you're lucky—but let's face it, how likely is that? On the other hand, dragging a suitcase across

town every time you go from one place to the other can make you feel homeless.

Some people get into the habit of saying "your mom's house" and "your dad's house." But those homes are yours, too. It's better to call them your home with your mom and your home with your dad.

When you have two homes, it's important to make sure you have a space of your own at both of them. It might not be your own room, but you do need your own bed, your own closet space, and spots to keep pictures and things that are important to you. You should be able to leave things in both places and know that the next time you come home, your belongings will still be where you want them. Discuss this with each parent and let each know what you need in order to feel at home. If it's OK with them, decorate your room at both places to make yourself comfortable there.

With your parents, figure out what you can duplicate and keep at both homes. It's reasonable to have a drawer of underwear and your basic toiletries at both places, for example, but it's a lot less likely that you'll have two iPods or two heavy winter coats.

Write out a simple checklist of things you'll need to take back and forth. Choose a convenient place in each home where you can put things you're going to take to the other home. It's a lot easier to pick up a pile than it

Schlepping your belongings back and forth between your two homes can get old in a hurry. It's much more comfortable to keep basic necessities in both places.

is to race around trying to think of everything when it's time to go.

Scrambled Schedules

Coordinating your activities and your social life with a court-ordered visitation schedule can cause challenges. If you're on a team or in an organization, give copies of its schedule to both parents so that they'll know when you need to go to practices or meetings.

One-time events are harder to plan. Keep communication open with both parents and let them know as soon as you're aware of a possible calendar conflict. Show that you do want to spend time with them and keep them aware of all your activities. If you do, they'll be more likely to understand when something special comes up and you'd like to make an exception to your regular visitation schedule.

Distant Relatives

There are two kinds of distant relatives. Some are distant in terms of family, such as your great-great-aunt or your mother's second cousin. You probably don't keep in touch with them anyway, so the divorce won't affect those relationships. But if Dad moves 800 miles (1,287 kilometers) away to take a new job, he becomes a "distant" relative. That's going to throw a big snarl into your regular every-other-weekend visitation schedule.

And what about your grandparents or family who live in other states? You shouldn't have to give up relationships that are meaningful to you just because your parents have split. It will take some creativity to figure out how you can still keep these special people in your life. You can start with e-mails, phone calls, and video chats, of course. For face-to-face visits, tell your parents that you miss seeing your grandparents or whoever it is and ask them to help you work out a visit.

House Rules

When you have two homes, it's a safe bet that you'll be living with two different sets of household rules. You can avoid a lot of trouble by remembering what's allowed in each home. For example, there may be different limits on how much time you can watch television or what shows you can watch. One parent may expect you to do your homework before dinner, while the other may insist that you're in charge of loading the dishwasher after meals. If you have different curfews at the two homes, you'll have to remember which is which when you go out with friends.

It can be easy to forget a rule and get in trouble. One solution can be to write down the rules at each home and keep the list handy.

One important note: Consequences for rule breaking will also vary between homes. However, the custodial parent should never "ground" you from your regularly scheduled visitation with your noncustodial parent.

Adapting over the Years

As you grow older, the challenges will change, but there will always be differences. When you get your

Technology such as e-mail and video chats can make it easier to stay in touch with friends and relatives, even if you move and can't see them as often in person.

driver's license, will there be different rules about using a car? If you get a part-time job after school, how will that affect your visitation schedule? The good news is that you can start right away to work with your parents on being flexible and considerate. That way, all of you can continue to adapt and be reasonable as your situation changes over the years.

10 Great Questions to Ask a Therapist or Counselor

1. Where will I live? Do I have to move away from my friends? Will I have to change schools? Will I be separated from my brothers/sisters?

2. How and when will I see the parent I don't live with? Do I have any say in the visitation schedule?

3. I'd really rather live with Mom/Dad. Will the judge listen to me?

4. Will I have to testify in court?

5. Will the visitation schedule mess up my activities or plans? What about birthdays, holidays, and vacations?

6. How will we have enough money to get along?

7. Is it possible that my parents will get back together again?

8. What happens if Mom or Dad gets married to someone else?

9. Can I still see my grandparents on both sides? What about my other relatives?

10. Does this mean I'm probably going to get a divorce when I grow up?

CHAPTER 4

This book isn't about your parents—it's about you. Still, your parents are a permanent part of your life, and it helps to have a good relationship with them.

It used to be that you knew your mom and dad. Maybe you had a great relationship; maybe it was just so-so. Maybe things were pretty rocky, but at least you knew what to expect. You knew when to push their buttons and when to lie low. You could read their moods. Now suddenly they've changed.

THEY'RE UNHAPPY, TOO

Once upon a time, your parents decided to get married. They had hopes and plans and dreams. They promised to spend the rest of their lives together. Now they must face the failure of that promise. If they're being hard on you now, it's because they're unhappy themselves. Unhappy people tend to dump their unhappiness on everyone around them.

Grown-ups Don't Always Feel Grown Up

Remember the "broken cookie syndrome"? It happens to adults, too. That means if your

When a married couple divorces, both partners usually feel like failures. Unhappy people tend to spread unhappiness. If your mom and dad are being hard on you, it's probably because they're so unhappy themselves.

mom screams at you for leaving wet towels on the bathroom floor, she may really be screaming because she had a huge argument with your dad that morning. It's childish, and it's not fair to you—but it happens.

A parent who feels overwhelmed may turn to his or her own parents for help. You could find yourself spending a lot more time with your grandparents or even living with them for a while as your parent tries to cope with this change in all your lives.

A small number of moms and dads are people who never really grew up themselves. They weren't ready to have children when they did. It

doesn't mean they don't love you, and it's not because of anything you said or did. They just weren't prepared for all that parenting involves.

Ways Parents React to a Divorce

Psychologist Constance Ahrons, who studies divorcing parents, found different types of relationships ranging from friendly to hostile. Your parents will fit somewhere along this spectrum:

- "Perfect Pals." It may seem hard to believe, but some parents are able to maintain a friendship after the divorce. They share the decision-making and parenting, and they do everything they can to make life easier for you.
- "Cooperative Colleagues." These parents are not friends, but they are able to talk calmly about decisions and make compromises when they disagree. The situation isn't ideal for you, but at least it's comfortable.
- "Angry Associates." Angry parents let their anger affect every aspect of their relationships. They are tense and dissatisfied. You find yourself constantly on the defensive to anticipate and avoid their rage.
- "Fiery Foes." These parents are not only angry; they're aggressive, constantly looking for ways to hurt each other emotionally. They try to involve you inappropriately—expecting you to take sides, for example, or messing up visitation in order to hurt the other parent. They don't mean to hurt you;

they're just so focused on each other that you can be hurt by the fallout.

- "Dissolved Duos." This fifth type is not really a relationship. After the divorce, these couples have no contact with each other. The custodial parent has complete control and responsibility; the other parent is not in the picture. The noncustodial parent will not be an active part of your life.

No matter where your parents fall on this spectrum, they're still your parents. They may not act like it, and at times they may even seem to forget, but they do love you in their own way.

HAVE YOUR PARENTS GONE CRAZY?

You already know that it can be hard to make good choices and decisions when you're emotionally vulnerable. This is as true for grown-ups as it is for you. While they're upset and anxious about the divorce, they may say and do things that seem completely out of character. A parent who's normally good-natured and cheerful may show signs of deep depression. A parent who's normally reserved and low-key may become loud and pushy or even take up risky habits.

Things Your Parents May Say

- "You're just like your father/mother." This phrase is usually said in an insulting tone when your parent is

Unhappy parents are likely to lash out at everyone around them. They don't mean to hurt you, but they're so focused on their own pain that they don't think about your feelings.

displeased with you. Such an accusation is doubly hurtful. First, it implies that your other parent is a bad person, which negates all your good memories and feelings about that parent. Second, it implies that you are a bad person, too. Of course you've picked up some mannerisms from each parent—the way your mom tilts her head when she laughs, perhaps, or your dad's good timing when he tells a joke. But you're not "just like" either parent, and you should be recognized and valued as an individual.

- "Your mother/father is a _____." The word in the blank may vary, but it won't be a compliment. You don't really want your mom and dad putting each other down to you, and you have a right to stop the conversation. The very worst form of this statement is "Your mother/father doesn't love you." That's not true. The parent who would say it is speaking from a place of hurt and anger and not thinking about your feelings. One response is to say, "Stop! It really hurts me to hear you say that."

- "Can you keep a secret?" A parent may start treating you as a friend and tell you things you're not comfortable hearing. This may have nothing to do with the divorce; it could be that your parent is simply lonely and wants to share things that one would normally tell a spouse. If you don't want to hear gossip about your parent's friends or private things your parent is doing now, you have the right to stop him or her. A phrase like "T.M.I." (Too Much Information) can be a clue that the conversation is crossing a boundary. No parent should depend on you for emotional support or as a substitute for adult friendship.

- "That's none of your business." A parent may get so tight-lipped that you're left without information that you have a right to know. For example, you have a right to be up to date on the divorce itself. If you ask, "When is the custody hearing?" the answer should be a date or at least, "It hasn't been set yet but should be in the next month." At times you might need to rephrase your question more appropriately. Asking if your dad has paid his child support this month gets into your mom's business, while asking if you can order your class ring yet is clearly your business. And of course, if you ask about things that should be private between your mom and your dad, sometimes that truly isn't your business.

Things Your Parents May Do

- Seem distant. A parent who is preoccupied with problems may pay less attention to you than you're used to. They might have to work more to make ends meet. They may seem to ignore your needs or have a difficult time discussing the divorce in general.
- Bribe you. A parent may become a "Mall Mom" or "Disneyland Dad," trying to buy your love by spending money on you. It can be tempting to take advantage of this sudden generosity, but it's not a healthy basis for a relationship.
- Put you in the middle. Parents who don't want to talk to each other may expect you to carry messages back and forth. They may quiz you to tell them what's going on in the other household. It's not fair of them to put you in the middle, and you have a right to refuse.
- Mess up visitation. A parent who suddenly changes a visit that's already scheduled or who insists that your belongings must stay "at home" when you go for a visit might be trying to cause problems for the other parent. A parent cannot forbid you to visit your other parent if the court has allowed that visitation.

HOW CAN YOU TALK TO YOUR PARENTS?

An old poem begins, "If you can keep your head when all about you are losing theirs and blaming it on you ..." These lines suggest a goal you can set for yourself during the craziness of your parents' divorce. You don't have to let it make you crazy, too.

Honesty

You want your parents to be honest with you. You can be honest with them as well. If they ask you how you are, tell them as much of your feelings as you're comfortable sharing. If you're sad or upset, it's OK to say so. Don't pretend things are fine if they're not, just to please your mom or dad.

Limits

If anyone tries to grill you about things you're not ready to share, it's OK to set limits. You should never be forced to carry messages back and forth between your parents so that they won't have to talk to each other. You should never be forced to spy on one parent for the other or to keep secrets from one for the other. If your parents try to use you as a go-between, you have a right to say no.

One or both of your parents may try to buy your affection with money, expensive gifts, or special vacations. This may be tempting, but it's better to focus on having a good personal relationship.

Conversation Starters

- Your activities. Even though your parent may not say so, he or she misses being involved in your life. Mention something that has happened at school, something fun you've done with friends, or an upcoming activity you're looking forward to. Share a bit of your daily life.
- Movies, TV, books. Do you and your parent enjoy the same TV shows? Talk about the most recent episode. Have you seen a good movie lately or read a good book? Recommend it, saying why you think your parent would enjoy it.
- Suggestions for future visits. Is there something you used to enjoy doing with your parent, some special place to go or fun activity or hobby you used to share? Ask when the two of you can do that again.
- Cars, college, careers. Speaking of the future, you can ask for advice about all kinds of things. What kind of car would your parent recommend for your first car? What's it like to go to college? If you've started thinking about what you'd like to do after you finish school, share that with your parent and ask for advice. You don't have to follow the advice, but it will help you think about these topics, and your parent will be pleased that you asked.
- Family history. You don't have to talk only about the present and future. Ask about your parent's childhood or family. What's a funny memory about your grandparents? What pets did your parent have growing up? Share some of your own happy memories. Talk about things that really interest you, and you'll get to know each other better as individuals.

Respect

You may not respect the way your parents are acting, but they are still your parents. The military has a phrase, "Salute the uniform." Soldiers are required to salute officers who outrank them. If a soldier does not respect an officer as a person, the soldier still salutes to show respect for the uniform the officer is wearing. In the same way, you can be respectful to your parents simply because they are your parents. Trust that in time, when the divorce is no longer freshly painful, they will be more reasonable.

Privacy

Remember that the divorce is between your parents, and you shouldn't be dragged into the messy details. Even if you find out that one of your parents cheated or was deliberately cruel to the other, that's still between them. Try not to let their private problems influence your relationship with either one of them.

Focus

When you talk with a parent, be clear about your own feelings and needs. Don't be sucked into discussing your parent's personal problems. Keep the discussion focused on how a specific problem or situation affects you. Really listen to your parent's response. Don't be planning your next statement until you take time to consider what he or she has to say. You may need to

It can be stressful when both of your parents come to one of your activities. It's OK to ask them to set aside their differences temporarily so that you can enjoy your event.

continue the conversation later, after you've had time to think things through.

When Your Parents Are Together

It's hard to be around parents who are feuding. They may argue and insult each other. They may refuse to speak at all. You have the right to ask them to call a truce when they are with you. When you have a special event and want both parents to attend, you can tell them the occasion is important to you and ask them to be polite to each other for your sake.

Whenever you can, use positive phrases. Avoid saying negative statements such as "you always" and "you never."

Visiting your noncustodial parent won't feel so strange if you keep in touch between visits. One way is to teach your parent how to use tools such as social media.

These will make your parents feel defensive. Instead, describe what you would like: "I need your help to make this a happy birthday."

The Parent You Visit

You used to live with this parent, and suddenly you feel like a guest in a strange place. Conversation can feel awkward and unnatural. Before a visit, think of two or three things you could talk about, to get the ball rolling.

In between visits, you can stay in touch by e-mail, snail mail, webcam, videos, phone calls, and even social networking. You might want to make a scrapbook or memory box of things you do together.

If you don't see your noncustodial parent as often as the visitation schedule would allow, and you would like more regular visits, it's OK to mention it. Don't make accusations, pressure your parent to "come home," or say hurtful things like, "Don't you love me?" A simple "I miss you. I'd like to see you more often" is a good start.

As strange as it sounds, divorce can help bring you closer to one or both parents through more open discussions. Perhaps you can plan activities with each parent as part of the healing process. In time, you can have a separate but strong and loving relationship with each parent.

Having separate one-on-one time with each parent can help draw the two of you closer together. You haven't really lost a parent; you're building a new relationship—different but special.

WHAT WILL HELP?

Even when things seem blackest, you always have the possibility of hope. Your parents' divorce may be all-consuming today, but you can reach out for help to make tomorrow better.

BE GOOD TO YOURSELF

Sometimes it's OK to be selfish. When you're struggling and feel abandoned, you can take initiative for meeting your own needs.

Have a Support Group

It's hard to know where to go for help when you no longer feel comfortable at home. Even when your parents are too wrapped up

When your relationship with your parents seems to be falling apart, it's good to reach out and talk with a few other people who care about you and will listen without judging.

in their own situation to be much comfort to you, other people can be a source of support.

You may want to share with a few close, trusted friends, especially if they've been through the divorce of their own parents. Parents of your friends can also be good to talk with, whether they have experienced a divorce or not.

Do you have brothers or sisters? You can support each other during this difficult time. Neighbors and close relatives may also have a sense of what you're experiencing and be able to provide a safe place to talk.

If you have pets, you know how loving and accepting they can be. Sometimes just cuddling a dog or cat that loves you unconditionally can make you feel better.

This is not the best time to start a new romance. If you already have a boyfriend or girlfriend, that person can be supportive. Try not to let neediness interfere with your relationship.

You may feel the need to talk with a professional. A licensed therapist, counselor, or social worker will have experience helping children of divorced parents. Also consider a clergyperson or youth leader in your faith community.

Own Your Feelings

Psychologist Suzy Marta emphasizes that you must mentally grasp what has happened and make sense of your loss in order to deal with it. She recommends telling your story—out loud—over and over. Getting your feelings out in the open helps you gain power over them. Each retelling lets you see new aspects and gain more insights. Gradually, you will accept it as real and come to terms with it.

Keeping a journal can be a way to stay in touch with how you feel from day to day. Rather than focusing only on the negatives, you can also use time alone to figure out your strengths. Imagine the future

Bottled-up feelings can suddenly explode at the worst times. Recognizing and expressing what you feel—to another person or in the privacy of a journal—helps relieve the pressure.

What to Do If There Is Violence in the Home

If you ever feel unsafe—if one of your parents begins hitting, abusing, throwing things, or making threats toward you or anyone else in the home—you need to tell someone. This is not the time to tough it out. Get help.

If the danger is immediate, call 911.

For information about services available in your area, call the U.S. National Domestic Violence Hotline: 1-800-799-7233.

Remember that other people can search the history on your home computer. If you plan to contact a helpline or website, it might be safer to use a computer at school, a library, or a trusted friend's house.

you want for yourself and reflect on ways to make it possible.

When you feel really down, it's OK to cry.

Take Care of Your Body

You may not have much appetite, but it's still important to eat well. Emotional distress can lead to eating disorders, which in turn make you feel more distressed. It's a vicious cycle you don't want to start. Eat a variety of foods across the food groups, in moderation. Use common sense: Don't skip breakfast or any other meals, eat fruits and vegetables every day, and take it easy on junk food. Be sure to drink several glasses of water every day because being dehydrated harms both your body and your brain.

Depression and grief can cause insomnia. It's important to get enough sleep. Lack of sleep makes it hard for you to concentrate, and you can become clumsy and emotional. Try to set up a consistent sleep schedule of going to sleep and getting up at the same time every day. If you need medication to help you sleep, avoid over-the-counter sleeping pills. Instead, ask your family doctor for a prescription that's right for you.

You may be vulnerable to substance abuse at this time. Don't be tempted to use drugs or alcohol to feel good. The effects are temporary, and the side effects can be serious, even deadly.

Stay Active

The kind of activity that will help you feel better depends in part on your personality. You might enjoy joining a sports team or entering into informal games at a public park. Perhaps you'd rather go running alone in the morning.

Surprisingly, sometimes the best way to feel better is the opposite of what you normally do. If you're usually a quiet person, try fifteen minutes of vigorous exercise. If you're the athletic type, consider a calming activity such as deep breathing or yoga.

When stress hits, take a time-out. Sometimes the best response is a relaxing activity that can take your mind off your problems. Get a massage. Take a long

bath. Listen to music or play a musical instrument of your own. Go to the library and check out favorite kids' books you remember from when you were little. Swing or slide at a playground.

Professional Counseling

When your family is coming apart, an outside professional can help everyone through the rough spots. You don't have to go it alone.

A psychologist is an expert in understanding what's happening in your head. He or she can talk with you one-on-one, letting you express your feelings in a safe, confidential situation. The psychologist's feedback can help you understand your feelings and make sound decisions.

A social worker is specially trained at understanding and improving the conditions in which people live. This is someone who can work with your family on solving specific problems related to life skills and living conditions.

A family counselor is an objective listener who deals with everyone in your family, not just individuals. Often counseling continues for weeks or months so that the counselor can watch the family dynamics grow and change, offering suggestions and solutions. The counselor acts as an intermediary between and among family members.

Whether you do it alone or with others, physical activity is good in lots of ways. Being active burns off stress. It keeps your body healthy. It can build your self-esteem.

When families are having trouble communicating, a professional family counselor will listen objectively, without judging, and help the family members build or rebuild healthy relationships.

Over time, professional counseling or therapy can help family members find a new balance to their rules, roles, and relationships.

FORGIVENESS

You've probably seen the smooth, polished, thumb-sized rocks that have a word carved into them. They're sold under different names such as "worry stones" or "serenity stones." The idea is to keep one in your pocket where you can rub it with your fingers when you're feeling stressed or upset, and it will remind you to be at peace or not to worry. The words include qualities such as "courage," "imagi-nation," faith," "strength,"

"hope," "peace," "forgiveness," "charity," and of course "love."

A gift shop owner once commented that these stones generally sell very well. The only one that didn't was the stone marked "forgiveness." He had many of those left over.

Why don't people want to forgive? Forgiveness is often seen as a sign of weakness. Sometimes we'd rather get mad. When we've been hurt, it can be natural to want to get even. The trouble with this is that staying mad or seeking revenge makes the hurt last longer.

Author Lewis B. Smedes talks about why and how to forgive. His book *Forgive and Forget* has the subtitle "Healing the Hurts We Don't Deserve." That certainly describes your situation when your parents divorce. It hurts, and you don't deserve it. In fact, the hurt is made worse because it's your own parents who have hurt you—the parents who are supposed to love, protect, and take care of you.

Smedes is realistic about the hurt and anger. He is also realistic about how to heal. He has identified four stages of healing, much as Dr. Kübler-Ross identified stages of grief.

The first stage is hurt. There's no getting around it; you have to go through it. Seeing your parents split up hurts in many ways. The pain is personal: This isn't

It takes true courage and strength to forgive someone who has hurt you. Forgiveness may take a long time, especially if you didn't deserve the hurt, but it's the only way to heal completely.

feeling sorry for someone else; it affects you directly. The pain is unfair. You didn't do anything to deserve having your life turned upside down. The pain is deep; you feel it in your gut and in your bones, and your heart aches.

The second stage is hate. It's instinctive, a backlash against deep and unfair pain. And it's especially painful when you both love and hate the same person. The hate may be passive, a lack of feeling toward the person or a hint of malice that you can hardly admit to yourself. Or the hate may be aggressive, actively wishing harm to the person who has harmed you.

Don't confuse hate with anger. Anger is an energy that can be channeled into changing whatever makes us mad. Hate never makes things better. It's like a cancer that grows in us and makes things worse. Fortunately, when we recognize and face hate, it can be cured.

The third stage is healing. This is a slow process that may take a long time. Don't try to hurry the healing, or it may be incomplete. Stop thinking about the person as the one who hurt you and instead try to see the person as a fallible human being. When you can think of the person apart from the pain, you have begun to heal. Gradually allow yourself to forgive the person. Don't worry if you can't do it all at once; it

When you have lived through the pain and worked through forgiveness, you can build a new relationship with the person who hurt you.

may be years before you can forgive him or her, but once you do, you will feel a tremendous relief.

The fourth stage is coming together. Completely cutting off the person who hurt you will leave a hole in you. Part of the healing process is allowing him or her to still be a part of your life.

Forgiving is not forgetting. The divorce is part of your history now, and you will always remember it. But if you remember without forgiving, it will continue to hurt. Forgiving lets go of the pain and allows you to build a new relationship with each parent.

GLOSSARY

adrenaline A hormone that the body releases when it experiences a strong emotion, such as stress or excitement, and that increases heart rate, pulse rate, blood pressure, and energy.

advocate A specialist who speaks for the interests of another person; in custody hearings, an advocate speaks for a minor child so that the child will not have to appear in court.

broken cookie syndrome The phenomenon that happens when a minor incident seemingly causes a person to overreact, when the reaction is actually due to the accumulation of other incidents and stresses.

child support Money paid by a noncustodial parent to the custodial parent to help with the care and upbringing of a minor child.

clinical depression A state of depression so severe that it requires professional intervention, either because it has no obvious environmental cause or because the negative reaction to life experiences is more intense or prolonged than would usually be expected.

coping mechanism A method or strategy for dealing with a specific problem.

counselor A person who gives counsel or advice; a counselor may or may not be a trained therapist.

custodial parent The parent who has custody of a minor child.

custody Responsibility to care for someone; in cases of divorce, a legal duty to care for a child.

divorce The legal ending of a marriage.

family counselor A person who works with a family as a group, rather than with individuals, offering suggestions and solutions about family dynamics.

intermediary A person who acts as a go-between or mediator to settle disputes between other persons.

joint custody Custody in which both parents share responsibilities and obligations and make decisions together.

judicial separation A legal decree that splits a couple without ending the marriage bonds.

legal custody The right to make decisions about a child's education, medical treatment, religion, care, protection, and best interests.

noncustodial parent The parent who does not have custody of a minor child.

physical custody The right of a parent to have a child live with him or her.

primary custody Custody that reflects the parent with whom a minor child lives the majority of time.

psychologist A specialist in the science of mental states and processes, trained and educated to do psychological research, testing, and therapy.

separation An arrangement by which a married couple stops living together.

social worker A person trained and educated to work toward improving social conditions and promoting the welfare of children.

sole custody An arrangement in which one parent has full responsibility and makes all decisions for a child.

stepfamily A family formed when a parent marries a person who is not his or her child's other biological or legal parent.

supervised visitation Visitation that must take place in a neutral location or in the presence of a neutral third party, due to a high-risk or high-conflict situation.

support network A combination of people, organizations, agencies, and programs that together provide emotional and physical support to someone who is in serious difficulty.

therapist A person trained in the use of psychological or physical methods for helping people with problems.

trial separation Informal arrangement wherein a couple separates without legal proceedings.

visitation The right of a noncustodial parent to spend time with a minor child on a regular ongoing basis.

FOR MORE INFORMATION

Action Alliance for Children (AAC)
2150 Allston Way, Suite 400
Berkeley, CA 94704
(510) 982-6680
Website: http://www.4children.org

AAC works to inform, educate, connect, and inspire people who work with and on behalf of children. It provides useful, reader-friendly information on current issues, trends, and public policies that affect children and families.

Arizona Foundation for Legal Services and Education (AZFLSE)
4201 N. 24th Street, Suite 210
Phoenix, AZ 85016-6288
(602) 340-7366
Website: http://www.azflse.org

AZFLSE provides resources and programs for children, educators, and others who want to learn more about laws and the legal system.

Children's Rights Council (CRC)
1296 Cronson Boulevard, Suite 3086
Crofton, MD 21114
(301) 459-1220
Website: http://www.crckids.org

CRC is a national nonprofit organization that deals with custody issues and divorce reform. It works to support and strengthen families, working on behalf of children to make sure they have healthy relationships with both parents.

Child Welfare League of America (CWLA)

1726 M Street NW, Suite 500
Washington DC 20036
(202) 688-4200
Website: http://www.cwla.org

CWLA, a coalition of private and public agencies, supports children—especially those with backgrounds of abuse, neglect, or other disruptive influences—and families through various policies, initiatives, programs, and resources.

Dibble Institute

P.O. Box 7881
Berkeley, CA 94707-0881
(800) 695-7975
Website: http://www.dibbleinstitute.org

The Dibble Institute is an independent, not-for-profit organization that provides resources to help teens and young adults learn healthy relationship skills.

Family Kind

178 Columbus Avenue
Box 230355
New York, NY 10023
(646) 580-4735
Website: http://www.familykind.org

Family Kind is a partnership between attorneys, mental health experts, mediators, parent coordinators, and other licensed professionals who help parents, teens, and children cope with the effects of divorce. Services include workshops, mediation, parent coordination, and classes.

Kids' Turn
(415) 777-9977
Website: http://kidsturn.org/kt

Kids' Turn offers workshops and resources for children and teens whose parents have separated or divorced or are in the process of doing so. The organization also offers curriculum models in divorce education targeted to various age groups, and its online program helps families facilitate healthy discussions.

National Clearinghouse on Families and Youth (NCFY)
Family and Youth Services Bureau
5515 Security Lane, Suite 800
North Bethesda, MD 20852
(301) 608-8098
Website: http://ncfy.acf.hhs.gov

NCFY is a service of the Family and Youth Services Bureau that provides free information about research related to the well-being of families and youth. The website includes a live-chat feature, Monday through Friday, 9 AM to 5 PM Eastern time.

National Network to End Domestic Violence (NNEDV)
1400 16th Street, Suite 330
Washington, DC 20036
(202) 543-5566

Website: http://nnedv.org

NNEDV is dedicated to ending domestic violence. It sponsors Safety Net: The National Safe and Strategic Technology Project to address how technology impacts the safety, privacy, and rights of victims and how to use technology to increase and maintain safety and privacy.

National Stepfamily Resource Center
c/o Department of Human Development and Family
   Studies
203 Spidle Hall
Auburn University
Auburn, AL 36849
Website: http://www.stepfamilies.info

The National Stepfamily Resource Center serves as a clearinghouse of information, linking family science research on stepfamilies and best practices for working with couples and children in stepfamilies. Resources include facts and FAQs about stepfamilies, summaries of stepfamily research, and training institutes for therapists, counselors, and family life and marriage educators.

Rainbows Canada
80 Bradford Street, Suite 545
Barrie, ON L4N 6S7
Canada
(877) 403-2733
Website: http://www.rainbows.ca

Rainbows Canada is an international not-for-profit organization that fosters emotional healing among children and youth grieving a loss. These losses, among others, include separation, divorce, death, incarceration, foster care, and military deployment.

StepFamily Foundation of Alberta
4803 Centre Street Northwest, Suite 201
Calgary, AB T2E 2Z6
Canada
(403) 245-5744
Website: http://www.stepfamily.ca

The Stepfamily Foundation of Alberta is a not-for-profit that provides a variety of resources to help stepfamilies address and work through the difficulties often faced by stepfamilies.

WEBSITES

Because of the changing nature of Internet links, Rosen Publishing has developed an online list of websites related to the subject of this book. This site is updated regularly. Please use this link to access the list:

http://www.rosenlinks.com/411/Divo

FOR FURTHER READING

Amos, Janine. *Divorce* (Changes). New York, NY: Windmill Books, 2009.

Becker, Helaine. *How to Survive Absolutely Anything*. Markham, ON, Canada: Fitzhenry & Whiteside, 2012.

Bergin, Rory M., and Jared Meyer. *Frequently Asked Questions About Divorce* (Teen Life). New York, NY: Rosen Publishing, 2012.

Berry, Joy. *Divorce* (Good Answers to Tough Questions). New York, NY: Joy Berry Books, 2010.

Blume, Judy. *It's Not the End of the World*. Reprint ed. New York, NY: Atheneum, 2014.

Bryfonski, Dedria. *Child Custody* (Opposing Viewpoints). Detroit, MI: Greenhaven, 2011.

Buscemi, Karen. *Split in Two: Keeping It Together When Your Parents Live Apart*. San Francisco, CA: Zest Books, 2009.

Cefrey, Holly. *Domestic Violence* (Violence and Society). New York, NY: Rosen Publishing, 2009.

Cook, Trish, and Brendan Halpin. *Notes from the Blender*. New York, NY: Egmont USA, 2013.

Dessen, Sarah. *Along for the Ride: A Novel*. New York, NY: Viking, 2009.

Espejo, Roman, ed. *Custody and Divorce* (Teen Rights and Freedoms). Detroit, MI: Greenhaven, 2013.

Holl, Kristi. *Patchwork Summer*. New York, NY: Atheneum, 1987.

Holyoke, Nancy, and Scott Nash. *A Smart Girl's Guide to Her Parents' Divorce: How to Land on Your Feet When Your World Turns Upside Down*. Middletown, WI: American Girl, 2009.

Justesen, Kim Williams. *The Deepest Blue*. Terre Haute, IN: Tanglewood Press, 2013.

Kiesbye, Stefan. *Blended Families*. Detroit, MI: Greenhaven, 2009.

Klein, Karen. *Broken Circle: Children of Divorce and Separation*. Seattle, WA: CreateSpace, 2013.

Langwith, Jacqueline, ed. *Divorce* (Opposing Viewpoints). Detroit, MI: Greenhaven, 2012.

Levete, Sarah. *Taking Action Against Family Breakups* (Taking Action). New York, NY: Rosen Publishing, 2010.

Levete, Sarah. *The Hidden Story of Family Breakups* (Undercover Story). New York, NY: Rosen Publishing, 2013.

Levin, Judith. *Depression and Mood Disorders* (Teen Mental Health). New York, NY: Rosen Publishing, 2009.

Mattern, Joanne. *Divorce*. Chicago, IL: Heinemann, 2009.

McDowell, Josh. *My Friend Is Struggling with Divorce of Parents* (Project 17:17). Ross-shire, Scotland: Christian Focus, 2009.

Michaels, Vanessa Lynn. *Frequently Asked Questions About Family Violence* (FAQ: Teen Life). New York, NY: Rosen Publishing, 2014.

Park, Barbara. *My Mother Got Married* (and Other Disasters). New York, NY: Yearling, 2007.

Peterman, Rosie L., Jared Meyer, and Charlie Quill. *Divorce and Stepfamilies* (Teen Mental Health). New York, NY: Rosen Publishing, 2013.

Porterfield, Jason. *Teen Stress and Anxiety* (Teen Mental Health). New York, NY: Rosen Publishing, 2014.

Quill, Charlie. *Anger and Anger Management* (Teen Mental Health). New York, NY: Rosen Publishing, 2009.

Reinhardt, Dana. *How to Build a House*. New York, NY: Random House, 2009.

Simons, Rae. *Blended Families*. Broomall, PA: Mason Crest Publishers, 2010.

Stern, Zoe, and Evan Stern. *Divorce Is Not the End of the World: Zoe's and Evan's Coping Guide for Kids*. New York, NY: Tricycle Press, 2008.

Stewart, Sheila, and Rae Simons. *I Live in Two Homes: Adjusting to Divorce and Remarriage* (Kids Have Troubles Too). Broomall, PA: Mason Crest, 2010.

BIBLIOGRAPHY

Ahrons, Constance, and Roy H. Rodgers. *Divorced Families: Meeting the Challenge of Divorce and Remarriage.* New York, NY: Norton, 1987.

Blaisure, Karen R., and Margie J. Geasler. "Children and Divorce." American Association for Marriage and Family Therapy. Retrieved March 15, 2014 (http://www.aamft.org/imis15/Content/Consumer _Updates/Children_and_Divorce.aspx).

Blaisure, Karen R., and Donald T. Saposnek. "Managing Conflict During Divorce." American Association for Marriage and Family Therapy. Retrieved March 15, 2014 (http://www.aamft.org/ imis15/Content/Consumer_Updates/Managing_ Conflict_During_Divorce.aspx.aspx).

Journeyworks Publishing. "Managing Your Stress." Exercise Your Stress Away, 1997. Retrieved March 15, 2014 (http://www.pamf.org/teen/life/stress/ managestress.html).

MacGregory, Cynthia. *The Divorce Helpbook for Teens.* Atascadero, CA: Impact Publishers, 2004.

Marta, Suzy Yehl. *Healing the Hurt, Restoring the Hope: How to Guide Children and Teens Through Times of Divorce, Death, and Crisis.* Emmaus, PA: Rodale, 2003.

Owens, Michael L., and Amy Gelman. *I'm Depressed. Now What?* (Teen Life 411). New York, NY: Rosen Publishing, 2012.

Peterman, Rosie L., Jared Meyer, and Charlie Quill. *Divorce and Stepfamilies* (Teen Mental Health). New York, NY: Rosen Publishing, 2013.

Smedes, Lewis B. *Forgive and Forget: Healing the Hurts We Don't Deserve.* San Francisco, CA: Harper and Row, 1984.

Stern, Zoe, and Evan Stern. *Divorce Is Not the End of the World: Zoe and Evan's Coping Guide for Kids.* Berkeley, CA: Tricycle Press, 2008.

U.S. Census Bureau. "American Fact Finder." Retrieved March 15, 2014 (http://factfinder2 .census.gov/faces/nav/jsf/pages/index.xhtml).

INDEX

A

abandonment, feelings of, 10–11
acceptance, as stage of grief, 35–37
Ahrons, Constance, 64
anger, 19, 53
  as stage of grief, 27–31, 37

B

bargaining, as stage of grief, 31–32, 37
betrayal, feelings of, 10
"bill of rights" for children of divorce/separation, 47–48
"bird's nest custody," 45–46
blame, 11, 19, 28
"broken cookie syndrome," 30, 61–62

C

coming together, as stage of healing, 94
conversation starters for talking to parents, 72
custodial/noncustodial parent, explanation of, 45
custody, explanation of, 45–46

D

decisions, making, 16
denial, as stage of grief, 24–25, 28, 37
depression, 85
  as stage of grief, 32–35, 37
  warning signs of, 33
divorce
  common reactions to, 10–18
  immediate changes, 38–42
  insensitive things people say, 18–21
  legal aspects, 42–48
  myths and facts about, 22–23
  ongoing challenges, 53–59
  statistics, 6–7, 22, 48

E

eating disorders, 84

ABOUT THE AUTHOR

Paula Morrow, Ph.D., is a youth services librarian at a busy public library in Illinois. A former magazine and book editor, she speaks at writers' conferences and presents workshops on writing for children and young adults. Morrow and her husband were for many years foster parents of teens diagnosed with emotional disorders.

PHOTO CREDITS

Cover, p. 1 Ned White/iStock/Thinkstock; pp. 4–5 altendro images/Stockbyte/Thinkstock; pp.8–9 Wavebreakmedia Ltd/Lightwavemedia/Thinkstock; pp. 12–13 Brankica Tekic/iStock/Thinkstock; pp. 14–15 kataijudit/Shutterstock.com; p. 20 SW Productions/Photodisc/Getty Images; pp. 26–27 altrendo images/Getty Images; p. 29 Todor Tsvetkov/E+/Getty Images; p. 31 Hill Street Studios/Blend Images/Getty Images; pp. 34–35 Tetra Images/Getty Images; pp. 36–37 Sanjay Goswami/iStock/Thinkstock; p. 39 Jupiterimages/Stockbyte/Thinkstock; pp. 40–41 sturti/E+/Getty Images; pp. 42–43 Alexander Raths/iStock/Thinkstock; pp. 50–51 Universal Images Group/Getty Images; p. 54 © iStockphoto.com/jabejon; pp. 58–59 Fuse/Getty Images; pp. 62–63 Alina Solovyova-Vincent/E+/Getty Images; pp. 66–67 Jupiterimages/Pixland/Thinkstock; pp. 70–71 JGI/Jamie Grill/Blend Images/Getty Images; pp. 74–75 Yellow Dog Productions/Iconica/Getty Images; pp. 76–77 Robert Daly/OJO Images/Getty Images; p. 78 Roberto Westbrook/Image Source/Getty Images; pp. 80–81 Stockbyte/Thinkstock; p. 83 Gary S Chapman/Photographer's Choice/Getty Images; p. 86 Smith Collection./The Image Bank/Getty Images; pp. 88–89 Bruce Ayres/The Image Bank/Getty Images; p. 90 Rhienna Cutler/E+/Getty Images; p. 92 Catherine Yeulet/iStock/Thinkstock.

Designer: Les Kanturek; Editor: Shalini Saxena